Agra

Poems and Ballads for Penny Readings

Original and Translated from the German

Agra

Poems and Ballads for Penny Readings
Original and Translated from the German

ISBN/EAN: 9783744776004

Printed in Europe, USA, Canada, Australia, Japan

Cover: Foto ©Thomas Meinert / pixelio.de

More available books at **www.hansebooks.com**

POEMS AND BALLADS

FOR PENNY READINGS

Original and Translated from the German

By AGRA

LONDON
WYMAN & SONS, 74-76, GREAT QUEEN ST.
LINCOLN'S-INN FIELDS
1883

CONTENTS.

Tel-el-Kebir	1
The Cross of St. George	4
The Alchymist	11
A Legend of the Alps	16
The Water-Logged Barque	27
The Poet's Home	38
Two Sonnets	43
The Legend of the Lac de Brêt ...	45
Luther and Freundsberg	52
The Midshipman and the Belle of the Ball ...	62
The Emperor and the Abbot	64
Norfall's Tower	74
Count Eberstein	82
Bertran de Born	85
The Young Lord and the Miller's Maid ...	89
The Youth and the Millstream	91
The Count de Greiers	95
Durand	99
The Wandering Bell	103
The Skeleton Dance	105
The Castellan De Coucy	108
Trusty Old Eckart	115
Harald	118
The Elves	122

TEL-EL-KEBIR.

[Lieutenant Harvey Goodwin Brookes, of the Gordon Highlanders, fell at Tel-el-Kebir pierced by four rifle-balls, leading his men with no other weapon than a spade, having lost his claymore in the sand. His body was found twenty yards beyond the first trench.]

Bury him here in the blood-stain'd sand,
   On the spot where he bravely fell;
With his broken spade in his cold right hand,
   The spade that he swung so well.

We halted our march through the starlit night
   One hour, the attack to form;
Gleam'd bright in his eye the battle light,
   And he burn'd for the coming storm.

The word to advance pass'd whisper'd down
    Our determined and silent ranks;
The bristling earthworks before us frown,
    A grey line of low sandy banks.

He had laid him down on the ground to rest,
    With his claymore by his side;
To the assault his kilted warriors press'd,
    Where he as a hero died.

In the dawning twilight his buried blade
    Was not at the moment found,
But he seized for the charge a sapper's spade,
    And the earthwork foremost crown'd.

The battle was won ere the sun arose—
    We found him among the dead—
In the thick of the fray, in the midst of foes,
    Had his hero spirit fled.

Then bury him here in the blood-stain'd sand,
  On the spot where he bravely fell;
With his broken spade in his cold right hand,
  The spade that he swung so well.

THE CROSS OF ST. GEORGE.

WHAT Englishman can ever look upon
St. George's Ensign from the masthead streaming—
The glorious Flag that thousand fights has won,
Foremost in War and Venture ever gleaming,
O'er Earth's most distant seas and headlands beaming,
The hallow'd emblem of our Liberty
Achieved while other nations still were dreaming,
Lock'd tight in tyrant bonds of slavery,
With scarce a thought, a wish, with no hope to be free?

Where is the man who e'er can look upon
That blood-red Cross upon its snow-white field,
Without a thrill of pride, a quicker run
Of tingling currents through the veins that yield
Transport ecstatic?—On the warrior's shield
It fiercely blazed eight hundred years ago,
When in the First Crusade the Normans wield
The Viking's sword against the Paynim foe,
And Saxon archers draw the dreaded English bow.

It waved across the sunny plains of France
Where Edward and the dauntless Harry led,
Not tenfold odds could stay its bold advance—
Cressy and Poictiers' fields bright lustre shed—
Beneath its folds noble and yeoman bled,
Gentle and simple, all like heroes fought
In stubborn rank, until the foeman fled—
Their valorous deeds were we as children taught—
Our infants proudly lisp the name of Agincourt.

From every port impatiently it leapt,
As beacons' flare the long-sought signal flash'd
That up the Channel the Armada swept,
And loud each tower and rocking steeple clash'd—
Breathless the world look'd on——The thunders crash'd,
And battle-fires and lightnings lit the main,
Straight at the Golden Flag the Red Cross dash'd,
And smoke hid both, and storm——But when again
The clouds dispersed, where was the vaunted might of Spain?

Then love of venture gallant spirits spurr'd
To dare all dangers for Old England's sake;
For ever flourish—each a household word,
Gilbert and Hawkins, Frobisher and Drake,
Heart-stirring names — Raleigh and generous Blake—
They won for us the Ocean's sovereignty,
Forced Commerce her old channels to forsake,
Made golden outlets for our industry,
Bearing St. George's Cross aloft from sea to sea.

Lo! Bannockburn and Flodden both forgot,
Under resistless Marlborough, fight their way
Now side by side, the Englishman and Scot
Far into Europe's heart, and gain the day.
Blenheim, Ramilies, Oudenard, and Malplaquet
Are victories with which the whole world rings—
And shining there with clear and silver ray,
On England's crimson Cross, St. Andrew's clings,
And vanquish'd in the dust the Golden Lilies flings.

The wedded Crosses conquer Hindostan,
To rule it wisely for her people's gain—
Complete what Alexander but began;—
While Britain's Ocean-sovereignty again
Great-hearted Nelson does for her maintain.
Victorious at the Nile, her Crosses fly—
Then Erin joins, to humble France and Spain,
Trafalgar sees the Red Cross hoisted high,
The Old White Flag 'neath which the Hero chose to die.*

---

* Nelson ordered the White Ensign to be flown at Trafalgar, —the Old Flag, as he fondly called it.

For see, the Irishman was not content
Till he had fasten'd on the two combined
His symbol.—Forth the perfect Flag is sent,
Its errand now to liberate mankind—
'Tis Ireland's joy the mighty Chief to find,
Great Wellington—he only can o'erthrow
The Tyrant, who so haughtily design'd
To force all nations 'neath his yoke to go.—
Our Crosses not in vain waved there at Waterloo!

Well has the world good cause indeed to bless
That Flag—and well may all the nations own
To Britain's blood-stain'd Cross indebtedness!—
It hurl'd the proud Usurper from his throne,
The Lord of Millions doom'd to pine alone;
It loosed the cursèd bonds of slavery,
And sanctified each spot where it was flown;
Could but the negro reach it he was free,
The Red Cross Banner gave the slave his liberty.

Americans! They were your sires that fought,
Above whom England's Red Cross proudly flew,
At Cressy, Poictiers, and at Agincourt;
Her boldest spirits sail'd the seas for you—
A share ye claim in Marlborough's victories too,
Kindred with those who turn'd the nation's fate
Both at Trafalgar and at Waterloo—
Your fathers' Flag will ye repudiate?
Nay! Let it all their sons once more confederate.

The Stars and Stripes your Empire's sign ye fly,
The Flag that mark'd your Independence won,
It cherish still, your Ensign rear on high—
But ye will add, ere many years have run,
Old England's Cross, as ye should first have done—
And it shall be the bond of unity
That shall make all the English peoples One—
Far mightier shall the noble Union be
Than Munroe ever dream'd, on land supreme and sea!

Then shall the world with envy look upon
St. George's Ensign from each masthead streaming—
The Flag that thousand glorious fights has won—
Foremost in Trade and Venture see it gleaming,
O'er Earth's most distant seas and headlands beaming,
The hallow'd emblem of our Liberty
Achieved while other nations still were dreaming,
Lock'd tight in tyrant bonds of slavery—
With scarce a thought, a wish, with no hope to be free.

THE ALCHYMIST.

The Alchymist sat in his turret alone,
    And he quaff'd of his golden wine;
All his life had he look'd for the wondrous stone,
    The philosopher's stone divine.
He had spent his resources, was now grown old—
That he had not found it need hardly be told.

But he did not despair, the older he grew
    The closer he studied his art,
And he hoped to be able his youth to renew,
    The stone would fresh vigour impart,
For, were it but found, men would no longer age;
And it was to be found—so taught every sage.

He had lived seventy years a solitary life
    In the hope of good times to come;
No friends had he made, nor yet taken a wife,
    Caring nought for the joys of home.
He would first find the stone, and then he would wed,
And revel in youth, wealth, and beauty, he said.

But, though neither wife nor yet friends he possess'd,
    Although he had now spent his store;
With a cask of rare wine was the old man blest,
    And with that what could he want more?
As he drank it his blood coursed fast through his veins,
His youth was renew'd, for it banish'd his pains.

And he lifted the goblet up to the light,
    And he dwelt on its golden hues,
And he ponder'd upon the sense of delight
    And the warmth that the draughts suffuse—
For it was the rarest, best vintage of wine,
Matured on the slopes of the sunny, blue Rhine.

And while he still gazed on the rich golden flood,
    There suddenly flash'd through his brain
A thought that set boiling his old sluggish blood ;
    The stone he would surely yet gain ;
For its essence was there in the goblet's shine,
And the stone that he sought was petrified wine.

So at once he set to the wine to congeal,
    And he wrought both early and late,
And he grudged time for sleep, and hurried o'er meal,
    But him mock'd still relentless Fate.—
At last, ere the cask was quite spent, I am told,
He made not the stone, but succeeded with gold.

But the wine was so rare, the gold it had made
    Was not half enough to suffice,
For a smaller cask of the wine it was paid,
    For that vintage had risen in price ;
And the more that he used the higher it went,
Till at last all the wine and the gold was spent.

But the stone was not found, and old age crept on,
    And death by starvation drew nigh,
And the Alchymist felt that his course was run,
    And he heaved a long, deep-drawn sigh,
To think the idea had not struck him before,
While life lay before him, unwasted his store.

My friends, ye will laugh at the Alchymist's craze,
    And hasten his folly to blame;
But do ye deserve, friends, yourselves better praise,
    And can ye equality claim?
He spent all his substance the stone for to find—
He yielded his life to do good to mankind.

But ye, in your sordid desire for mere wealth,
    Spend your lives in seeking for gold,
For selfish aggrandisement sacrifice health—
    And what gain ye when all is told?
From happiness here e'en on earth ye are far—
From future delights ye yourself thus debar.

List, then, to the sequel. An angel stood by,
    Took charge of the Alchymist's soul—
Wide open before them Heaven's pearly gates fly,
    Back the bars and the bolts all roll—
And the Alchymist finds there the long-sought stone,
And a gold'ner wine, far more rare than his own.

A LEGEND OF THE ALPS.

It chanced that I, on pleasure bent, one summer holiday,
High on an Alpine mountain-road, light-hearted took my way.

Impell'd, as wand'rers ever are, by scenery sublime,
I left the broad and levell'd road, a giddy path to climb.

Upon the mountain's snow-clad side, in dizzy altitude,
A monastery chapel hung, in frozen solitude.

And as I pass'd its open doors I stopp'd in
 sheer amaze,
A Magdalena, wondrous fair, held riveted my
 gaze.

I saw no more the mountain crests glowing in
 rosy light,
Art more than nature filled my soul with
 rapturous delignt.

I dare not as an artist may to cunning make
 pretence,
That altar-piece the beautiful fulfill'd in every
 sense.

I cannot even the spell describe it cast upon
 my soul,
Perfection in each detail glow'd, perfection
 crown'd the whole.

It seem'd in truth a living maid, the woman kneeling there,
Her tear-stain'd face upturn'd above, her hands tight clasp'd in prayer.

Her hair stream'd wild, her eyes were closed, she dared not look to Heaven,
Repentance struggled with the fear lest she were unforgiven.

Long, long I gazed upon the scene, until the verger came,
And then, at length, I turn'd to ask what was the painter's name.

"You well may ask," he answer'd me, "but I can not reply;
He was at least a master hand, that no man will deny.

" 'Tis strange that neither canvas bears, nor yet the
gilded frame,
Letters or mark by which were known the artist's
boasted name.

" But see in yonder corner, where the paint is worn
away,
There, in the years long since gone by, 'twas written,
so they say.

" And, if you like to list a while, the tale I'll briefly
tell,
What here before the altar stone once on a time
befell.

" A Bishop of our Holy Church this Chapel wish'd
to build,
And he desired an altar-piece by master-hand so
skill'd,

"That all who on his picture gaze, in heartfelt
    penitence,
May feel within their sorrowing souls of sins
    wash'd out the sense.

"But where, throughout all Christendom, might
    such a man be found?
He knew of only one, whose powers were far
    and wide renown'd.

"To him the holy prelate went—sad is the tale
    I tell,
The master led a godless life,—he was an
    infidel.

"Worse than a heathen, nothing more for Holy
    Church he cared,—
Never by prayer or penances for future weal
    prepared.

"And he at first refused outright the bishop's proud
  behest,
Nor could his gold persuade the man to yield to his
  request;

"Until the holy father spread, with ready guile, this
  rumour,—
That dread of failure, more than all, accounted for
  his humour.

"Then only he commenced the work, his genius thus
  attainted,
And with most wondrous, marvellous skill, this altar-
  piece he painted.

"But, in his pride and misbelief, beneath the golden
  frame,
He added words of blasphemy, below his written
  name.

"'Not for God's honour have I wrought; for the
glory of my art'—
He wrote in boastful letters there, with swelling,
haughty heart.

"Soon afterwards the master died, and mark well
now this story,
And God has power to turn, you'll find, even blasphemy to His glory.

"The painter died,—but in the grave no rest could
there *he* find,
Who in the course of his long life, ne'er work for God
design'd.

"Too late he strove, too late, in vain he painted
every night,
Until the mountain tops were tinged with dawn's first
rosy light.

"Although his wondrous genius still more pictures
    wrought so fair,
Vanish'd the ghostly colours all each morning into
    air.

"At the shrill cock's first warning crow, no longer
    dared they stay,—
Painter and canvas, easel, brush,—they faded all
    away.

"One day unto our mountain shrine a lonely woman
    came,
Her dress was worn, in rags, thread-bare, slowly she
    walk'd, and lame.

"Veiling her pale and careworn face, stream'd loosely
    down her hair,
And in the light of her wild eyes the fires of guilt
    were there.

"With falt'ring step and downcast look the narrow
   aisle she trode,
To Palestine, on penance bent, was stretch'd her
   weary road.

"She knelt before the Magdalene, and raised her
   gleaming eyes,—
Then all at once her soul burst forth in agonising
   cries,

"For in the weeping penitent above the altar
   shown,
She recognised the features traced, for they were once
   her own,

"When young and beautiful and gay she ever dainty
   fared,
And deck'd with costly gems and silks, the master's
   life she shared.

" There was the name beloved, and there, the golden
frame below,
Lay hid, as well she knew, those words, the cause of
all the woe.

" She fell upon the picture fair, her tears stream'd
down in rain,—
Could penance now no more avail, was penitence in
vain?

"All day before the altar-stone upon the ground she
lay;
At eve they came to lead her forth—her soul had
pass'd away.

" But in the picture corner, there, where yet the paint
is blurr'd,
Her scalding tears wash'd out the name, and that
vain-glorious word.

"The only written letters left, traced by the master's hand,
Beneath the massive golden frame, now, " for God's honour" stand.

"His work accepted thus by Heaven, he found at last his rest,
His soul, though here his name is lost, we dare to hope is blest."

THE WATER-LOGGED BARQUE.

(From an account in the papers.)

O'ER the blue waves of the heaving sea,
Under press of sail, she bounded free;
   The good ship's timbers were sound and tight,
And the skipper's heart beat high with glee.
   The wind was fair, and the sky was bright,
And the sailors sung loud in chorus their song,
They were homeward bound, and she plough'd fast
     along.

Verily, it was a noble sight
To view from the deck her canvas white;
   Pile upon pile still loftier spread,
Till the royals, glancing in the light
   Of the morning sun, high overhead,
To us hardly bigger appear'd than the hand,—
A mountain of snow inexpressibly grand.

While the foresail, bulging out before,
Swell'd in the breeze still more and more,
    Seem'd as it were a cathedral dome
Dark in the shadow.   The vessel tore
    Fast through the sea with a wake of foam,
And the splash of the waves on her side that beat
Made a gurgling music surpassingly sweet.

But too little time had we to gaze
On the snow-white canvas' towering maze,
    To list to the waves' bewitching sound.
The skipper look'd at the gathering haze,
    Then swept the horizon all around,
And he spoke to the mate, who sung out the hail,
" Get in the flying jib, and the gaff top-sail."

Succeeding orders then follow'd fast,
The mainsail was stow'd ere noon was past,
    And soon all hands were call'd from below,
The ship was stripp'd and close-reef'd at last :
    The weather changed, it began to blow,
And the sky was obscured by thin clouds like smoke,
As all of a sudden the hurricane broke.

And fiercer still the wild storm-blast grew,
The sea changed at once from deepest blue
    To a dark and greasy, sloppy green,
Then again like magic changed its hue,
    Nought but a white waste of foam was seen,
As squall follow'd on squall in infernal roar,—
Such an awful tumult I'd ne'er heard before.

The close-reef'd topsails to shreds were torn,
We thought each moment the masts were gone.
    Upon her beam ends the barque was thrown—
Who would have said such a glorious morn
    Could turn to wildest night ever known?
And who e'er would have thought but a few hours past
That such fearful weather for a week could last?

Each time that the watch was call'd, we thought
We'd seen the worst, as our berths we sought;
    That when again upon deck we came
A change of weather were surely wrought—
    But no, it raged still ever the same,
Still day after day the fierce hurricane blew,
Till, spent and worn out, oh how weary we grew!

Weary of bitter, cold, searching wind,
From which no shelter was there to find—
    Of the jumping seas and blinding spray,
The roar of the waves and storm combined.
    Each night how we long'd again for day,
But it seem'd to grow fiercer with dawning light,
Then we hoped for a change with the coming night.

A small storm trysail, and that set low,
Was all the canvas we dared to show,
    Hove to under which laid down was she;
Though now and then, when it ceased to blow,
    Or when lifted by a huger sea,
We righted a moment—but only to fall
Down flat with a jerk that electrified all.

And day by day the fierce blast kept on,
It seem'd the storm would never be done;
    Sometimes it lull'd, but only to breathe
For savager burst, and wilder run
    Of hissing waters that boiling seethe,
Of curling black billows with crests breaking white,—
Huge mountains of water, a terrible sight.

Word pass'd one morning we'd sprung a leak,
As the news went round blanch'd every cheek,
   And even the bravest held their breath—
For if it were true 'twere vain to seek
   Any longer escape from present death.
Exposed in the rigging—'twas awful to think
That our cargo was such *that she could not sink*.

We mann'd the pumps, but we work'd in vain,
We found every hour the water gain,
   Mocking our efforts, a stronger hold:
For days we kept up the fearful strain,
   Till the useless toil severely told,
We left off exhausted, worn out, one by one,—
The skipper admitted no more could be done.

And indeed 'twas time, the decks were swept
By every wave that in fury leapt
   Over the bulwarks in angry storm;
All huddled close on the poop we crept,
   The very picture of woe to form—
Lash'd tight to the railing, in misery to wait,
Half drown'd by the seas, a most terrible fate.

And then it was that we wish'd she'd sink,
But knew she would not—there on the brink
    Of death ever present days we stood,
    Lash'd to the poop-rails—the only link
      A paltry support of fragile wood
That connected us now with the human world,
While the angry white billows around us curl'd.

We heard ghostly shrieks and flapping wings,
It seem'd we had done with earthly things,
    We saw such sights as never before—
    Dread shapes that wild delirium brings,
      Sounds horrid above the tempest's roar.
It were hard now to think which was worst to bear,
The black terrors of night or the day's despair.

She lay like a corpse upon the sea—
Our strait more desperate could not be,
    As on the poop just above the wave
    We stood in our dire extremity;
      Shut in all round in an open grave—
For green walls of water on every side tower'd
And over our heads the black tempest pall lour'd.

THE WATER-LOGGED BARQUE.

I know not how long a time thus pass'd;
But the gale gave way one day at last,
   And our well-nigh sinking spirits rose:
We hoisted the flag half up the mast
   Jack-down—out bravely the signal blows—
As we rise on the waves we see through the spray
A vessel some leagues to the windward away.

Who can describe the desponding sense
That we were doom'd to experience,
   What anguish with ours can one compare?
It to depict I make no pretence—
   We watch'd her all day, she still was there;
But hove to it seem'd, for she kept the same spot,
It was plain to us all, they observed us not.

As for hours we strain our aching eyes
To keep up our hopes the captain tries:
   "Better our chance with the coming night,
Our flare will show in the darken'd skies,
   They will not fail to see a blue light!"
He spoke thus to cheer us, we needed it sore,
For lower our spirits had sunk than before.

We got together a heap of wood,
And dried some splinters as best we could;
    Once lit, the breeze soon blew up a flame,
And round the blaze more hopeful we stood—
    No answering gleams from the distance came,
Our blue lights were burn'd, and our flare died away—
How we peer'd through the gloom, and long'd for the day!

Voices at times we fancied we heard,
And cheer'd each other with joyful word,
    Listening and watching the long night through;
But nought they proved,—the cry of a bird,
    The rigging's hum, as fiercer it blew—
Still we caught at each sound with a maddening pain,
For our nerves were now stretch'd to the breaking strain.

At length, just before the break of day,
I made out a red light's brilliant ray,
    And loudly we shouted at the sight;
It came and went—at last died away;
    But soon we saw in the morning light
A big vessel approaching fast under steam,
Distant less than a mile on the weather beam.

We crowded all to the windward side,
And brandish'd our arms and stretch'd them wide,
   And shouted and shriek'd as though we fear'd
   We might even yet be still more tried;
   For she would pass on the course she steer'd,
And unless we show'd them how many we were,
They might leave us to die without further care.

But see, they have turn'd her head our way,
She comes down slowly in clouds of spray,
   Pitches and rolls in the heavy sea—
   As though, unwilling to yield its prey,
   The ocean swell'd in impotency,
The rescuer seeking in vain to o'erwhelm—
But she ranges abreast as she puts down her helm.

A large lifeboat comes, by brave men mann'd,
Dext'rously steer'd by a fearless hand,
   Now carried aloft—now pitching low—
   Upon the taff-rail we waiting stand—
   Not slight is her risk; a single blow
Would dash her to atoms upon the poop's side,
And drown her brave crew in the wild seething tide.

We must jump, they shout, and one by one,
In no other way can it be done;
 We must watch our chance and boldly leap,
As under our stern the boat comes on,
 Ere carried off by the next wave's sweep,
The lifeboat is borne to the leeward away—
We must seize the moment, and risk it, they say.

'Twas toilsome work for the gallant crew,
Their muscular arms had much to do
 To pull to windward as each man leapt;
But their English hearts were mettle true,
 Doggedly still to their task they kept;
They knew nothing of toil, there were lives to save,
Nor thought of the risk of a watery grave.

Brave fellows they, and while England boasts
 Such gallant crews round her stormy coasts,
 Full half the terrors of wrecks are fled,
And she may scorn an invader's hosts;
 On Britain's soil they would never tread,
For the men who for lifeboat work volunteer,
Like their fathers of old, know nothing of fear.

They braved for two hours that raging sea—
And a wilder flood there scarce could be—
   Until we all had happily sprung;
And when our captain—the last was he—
   Leapt into the boat, a loud cheer rung,
Rung echoing over the waves far and wide,
As they headed her round for the steamer's side.

We reach'd her safely without a check,
And soon lost sight of that awful wreck;
   And thankful we were again to feel
Springing beneath us a buoyant deck,
   So different from the sickening heel
Of the wave-beaten hull we had left behind;
I shudder, e'en now, when I call it to mind.

Since then in many a wreck I've been,
Hung more than once life and death between,
   On desert island been cast away,
Ship in mid-ocean on fire have seen—
   But of all I've pass'd through in my day,
That most miserable time bears the blackest mark,
Far the worst of all was the water-logg'd barque.

THE POET'S HOME.

WHERE shall the Poet seek on earth his home,
   Whom Heaven itself would scarcely long contain,
Whose restless soul from thence would wish to roam?
   Not even in bliss at rest can he remain;
Fleeting his genius as the storm-toss'd foam,
   His soaring spirit space can not enchain,
His song all bounds, all barriers doth refuse;
What home, himself contented, would he choose?

Will it be found amid the city's hum,
   His life-task there the study of mankind,
Where countless faces ever go and come,
   And most but mirror to a sordid mind;
Where Nature's joyous voice perforce is dumb,
   Where all to aught but gold and gain are blind?
There can the Poet have no dwelling-place,
Where man has marr'd the earth's fair, smiling face.

Will he find rest in desert vast and lone,
    Amid the relics of an age gone by,
'Mid broken shafts and pillars overthrown
    Which once tower'd upright to a brazen sky,
Where the parch'd sands are yet with fragments strown
    Of temples marvellous in immensity?
Their mythic tales his soul do not delight,
He must e'en elsewhere wing his fancy-flight.

Beside some mighty river's inpent stream,
    With rocks and gloomy pine-woods overhung,
That scarce at mid-day even the sun's warm beam
    Is ever on the rushing waters flung—
A dazzling ray, a passing, fitful gleam—
    A spot that folk-lore long ago has sung,
Of gnomes, and wraiths, and goblins dread the haunt,
Whose powers of mischief they not idly vaunt?

Or by the placid lake's clear, vast expanse
   By snow-clad mountain barrier vainly hemm'd,
Upon whose moonlit beach the fairies dance,
   Whose wavelets are by mermaid bosoms stemm'd,
Where jutting rocks out in the flood advance
   In jewell'd glory by the sunlight gemm'd?
Useless, alas! to him the fairy-lore,
Gnomes, goblins, mermaids, long have left the shore.

Majestic into heaven the Jungfrau towers,
   Ice-chastely draped in everlasting snows,
Veil'd by the storm-cloud's mist which darkly lours,
   From frozen brow to freezing bosom flows—
Cold and repellent are her wintry bowers,
   Even when her face with sunset blushes glows—
Terrific Grandeur, chilling Chastity,
O'erpowering sense of dread Eternity.—

Must he then seek among the orient seas
    A home her frigid altitude denies;
Where, wafted from the incense-breathing trees,
    Their perfumes blending, scented odours rise;
Where balm is borne on every fresh'ning breeze
    At morn and eve beneath the twilight skies;
Where all combines to kindle soft desire,
And kindled once, to ever fan the fire?

Or on the dreamy shores of sunlit isles,
    Where coral reefs rise out an amber sea;
Where languid Nature ever wanton smiles,
    The soul bewitching with her poetry;
Where dark-eyed Beauty meltingly beguiles
    Beneath the palm-grove's high-spread canopy?
All lures in vain to rest, and love, and ease—
His thoughts are fix'd on higher things than these.

Nay! on the summit of some wave-lash'd crag,
  Rising from out the foam so sheer and steep,
Whence ever proudly waves Old England's flag
  In red-cross grandeur far across the deep—
Fray'd by the storm-wind's blast the tatter'd rag
  O'er subject Ocean haughty guard doth keep,
Out on the breeze a crimson streamer flowing,
High in the clouds with beacon's splendour glowing.

There, if the Poet's soul can ever rest,
  There may, methinks, his teeming fancy dwell :
As the Past's mighty memories crowd his breast,
  A mightier Future there he will foretell ;
There may he end his restless, ceaseless quest,
  Roused by the storm, and lull'd by calm's soft swell ;
There shall he give his genius ample play—
Thence soar aloft on Heaven's eternal ray.

TWO SONNETS.

(1880.)

Nay, say not that Old England's race is run,
  Our load of Empire more than we can bear,
  No longer now can Britons do and dare—
Faint-hearted cravens! It is but begun.
The Anglo-Saxon Empire shall be One,
  United shall be many Empires there!
  Of this no true man should at all despair,
Far nobler deeds than ever yet were done,
And victories—though bloodless—far more great
  Than Roman—aye, or British annals tell—
For our United Empires still has Fate
  Reserved—One English speech will all compel,
Kingdoms, Republics to confederate
  In one grand Union wheresoe'er we dwell.

II.

The times are bad—can not be worse, ye say,
    And England's long ascendant star has set.—
    Hard times should not despondency beget!
'Tis darkest just before the dawning day,
But as we know the sun's all-piercing ray
    Will soon dispel the gloom, we do not fret;
    Our fathers harder times with courage met,
And we their sons will fling despair away!
If England's star—which I do not allow—
    Were set, there's still for us a rising sun;
Our heritage is glorious, anyhow.
    Vast continents we still may overrun;
And though our Empires are divided now,
    We Anglo-Saxons yet will all be One.

THE LEGEND OF THE LAC DE BRÊT

(NEAR LAUSANNE).

A WIDOW sat at the sunset hour
    Alone in the trellis'd shade,
Where still on the vine-leaves of her bower
    The fading sunlight play'd.

It was a cottage poor and mean,
    Its porch but a rough oak-bough,
But the well-kept floor and the walls were clean,
    And the cottage is standing now.

'Twas built on the road-side, near the gate,
    Some hundreds of years ago,
Where a city rear'd in ponderous state
    Defences against the foe.

Yet of that city vast and proud,
    Of its walls and turrets grey,
Of its massive gates and its thronging crowd
    Nothing is seen to-day.

The cottage stands on a green hill-side,
    On a pleasant, sunny steep,
But the city is sunk beneath the tide
    Of a mountain lakelet deep.

A stranger once to the city came,
    In the old grey time of yore,
He preach'd with power, for his words were flame;
    They turn'd him from door to door.

Worn out by his one persistent cry,
    They thrust him out the gate,
Threatening all with direst penalty
    Who on his needs should wait.

Thus nowhere, even in the poorest inn,
    Could he more a harbour find;
The townsmen, wholly given to sin,
    His message aye declined.

No longer in the market-place
    Could he scant victuals buy,
But still he preach'd the means of grace,
    "Repent! Repent!" would cry.

But in her cottage poor and lone
    The widow harbour'd him,
Though with suffering she was feeble grown,
    And her sight long since was dim.

And thus the months sped quickly by,
    Till a year had pass'd away;
Since the stranger first had raised his cry
    Had pass'd a year and a day.

The widow sat at the sunset hour
    Alone in the trellis'd shade,
Where still on the vine-leaves of her bower
    The fading sunlight play'd.

She waited there, and waited long,
    But the preacher did not come;
Hush'd was the city's busy throng,
    Still the stranger came not home.

But as the sun's last lingering rays
    Kiss'd the mountain's blushing cheek,
And the day gave place to twilight haze,
    She arose her guest to seek.

Slowly, and fill'd with sickening dread,
    She press'd on t'wards the gate,
Where the frowning ramparts overhead
    Foreshadow'd the preacher's fate.

But ere the drawbridged moat she trod,
    She turn'd, for she heard her name;
The Crucified, the Son of God
    In a radiant vision came:

"Not, daughter, in yonder town," He said,
    "Will he whom you seek be found;
Who for My cause his blood hath shed
    Is among My martyrs crown'd.

What for him for My sake thou hast done
    Thou hast even done for Me,
And now his race on earth is run
    I will requite it thee."

The vision faded in glorious light,
    The widow homeward turn'd;
And an awful fate befell that night
    The town which its Saviour spurn'd.

His servant had pleaded with wondrous power
  On that, the last day of grace ;
As the sun went down at the evening hour
  He died in the market-place.

They had tortured him there at the cruel stake
  Long hours through the hot noontide,
But he bore it all for his Master's sake
  Who for him was crucified.

*   *   *   *   *   *

The sun arose in a tranquil sky :
  No city more was seen,
No house but the widow's, standing by
  A lake where the town had been.

That cottage is standing there to-day
  By the placid waters' side,
And the mountain-peaks on the surface play
  Morn and eve in the mirror'd tide.

The fisher oft in the summer time
    In the dreamy noontide afloat,
As he hears a sound like a bell's sweet chime
    Peers down in the depths from his boat.

And he sees, many fathoms deep in the wave,
    Church-spires and embattled walls,
Where the city sleeps in its crystal grave
    Till the Judgment-trumpet calls.

LUTHER AND FREUNDSBERG.

[George of Freundsberg was one of the most distinguished generals in the Imperial army, and was the author of several improvements in the military system. He contributed greatly to the victory at Pavia; and a year afterwards raised, by pledging his estates, a force of 12,000 men, and thus enabled Charles of Bourbon to march upon and storm Rome. Bourbon fell in the breach, being the first to mount it, but the city was taken and sacked, and the Pope was kept a prisoner in the Castle of St. Angelo for seven months. Freundsberg was a man of great strength, and his deeds of personal prowess were greatly celebrated in his day.]

THE Emperor holds at Worms imperial state:
   Electors, margraves, dukes the chamber throng;
Archbishops, bishops, abbots, nuncios wait,
   While slowly winds the cavalcade along,
The coming of a Monk, whose pending fate,
Whose death-doom shall give peace to Christendom
And vassal all the world again to Rome.
Ambassadors from England, France, are there,
   Late from the pageant of the Cloth of Gold;

Their monarchs Papal honours fettering bear
With lavish splendour through all Europe told.
Magnificence of pomp not now their care ;
Defender of the Faith—Most Christian Majesty—
For loftier titles still the haughty rivals vie.

And Charles, the mighty Charles himself, is throned,
Imperial arbiter in courtly pride,
That Charles, whom Old and New World sovereign
own'd,
By him must yon poor wordy Monk be tried,
Tremendous issues he must there decide.
The power of Papal Rome yon Monk hath dared to
beard,
The standard of reform enthusiastic rear'd,
And of his bold self-will appear'd
His course to justify :
With dauntless front, in person dared to plead
Against the encroaching errors of that creed
That Pope and Kaiser hold,
Beneath whose banner sovereigns are enroll'd,
In whose defence these haughty kings would die.

Princes, and counts, and barons of the realm,
 The pomp and power of all the German land,
Statesmen and councillors who guide her helm,
 And Deputies from her Free Cities stand
  On either hand;
Imperial soldiery, Italians, Spaniards proud,
The portals of the hall, the ante-chambers crowd.
 Without, a mighty multitude
  Had the whole morn long stood,
 Eager to gaze their fill upon the man,
  The lowly Mansfeldt's miner's son,
Who all unaided his career began,
 Full tilt at Rome had dauntless run,
 And all alone the victory won;
  Who by the shock
Of thunder'd Truth's invective fiercely hurl'd
 Had shaken to its base the vaunted rock
Where sat enthroned the pontiffs of the world;
And now was come to argue out his cause
 Before his Kaiser, and in Europe's sight,
Relying on Germany's princes and her laws,
 And on his God to aye maintain the right.

"He comes—he comes!" is echoed down the street
In sounds confused, with rush of speeding feet,
As in the narrow lane, hedged bright with flashing spears,
Far in the distance now the Herald first appears,
 The Marshal of the Empire,—then the man
Whom all fast flock to see, to meet his death-doom nears.
 "He comes!" from every side the people ran;
"He comes, he comes!" fast flow'd the eager crowd.
In vain "Make way!" the soldiers shouted loud,
 The narrow lane is block'd,
 For faster still the people flock'd.
Forgotten Kaiser now, electors, prelates all,
In glad tumultuous shout the people "Luther" call;
 Till with the swell its high-peak'd gables rock'd,
And the long sound-wave surged within the Judgment hall.
 Herald and Marshal, Monk, are hemm'd
  Fast in the people's wild embrace,
 And, since the tide can not be stemm'd,
  Stand still and motionless a space,
  Then seek, since idle is delay,
  To reach the hall by other way.

The Herald orders, suddenly the door
    Of the first house next by is open thrown,
And while the tumult swells in deafening roar
    Enter the Herald, Marshal, Monk alone,
Who thus, ere can the crowd their purpose guess,
Escape the people's ever-gathering press.
By secret passages and garden-ways
    The Herald and the Marshal lead,
But the fond mob, more eager yet to gaze
    On the bold Champion of the Gospel-creed,
    Into the houses, through the gardens speed,
        And thread the alleys' maze ;
While the more venturous up the gables climb
To catch a glimpse of him for one short second's time.

While still assuring shouts re-echo loud
    As from all sides the countless thousands flock,
    Till the tall towers and spires vibrating rock ;
While all their windows wealthy burghers crowd,
    And sympathising throngs the roadways block ;
        The little band
        Once more is brought to stand:

Louder and louder swells the din,
    Although the town hall's gain'd,
    Its very threshold even attain'd,
    They cannot enter in,
Until the guards by force a passage clear,
And hold the people back with pike and spear:
Now courage, doughty Monk! the last dread goal is near!

    And, truth, he needs it all,
His spirit's utmost force, his readiest mind,
Prompt wit and judgment, answers well design'd,
Composure, and unbending stedfast will,
His lofty mission dauntless to fulfil,
As now the doors disclose the solemn council-hall.

    But ere the antechamber's pass'd,
Ere he is usher'd in the presence dread,
    Full many a kindly look is cast,
And cheering words of comfort said;
    And at the last,
Last moment as he enters there,
A brave knight bids him not despair.

'Twas George of Freundsberg, who has thus attain'd
    Far greater fame
By this one speech than all his victories gain'd,
    And more enduring crown;
Associate with the great Reformer's name
    His shall be ever handed down.
"Good Monk, good Monk!" the war-worn soldier cried.—
In many a field his courage had been tried,
    In many a desperate fray
His prowess and his skill had turn'd the doubtful day;
    But never yet when at the head
    Of charging squadrons he the conflict led,
    And in his stirrups standing high,
    With loud, exulting battle-cry,
    Cheer'd on his men to victory,
Had e'er the veteran spoke a truer word,
    Or one with consequence more fraught;
To greater issues ne'er had waved his sword
    Than his kind greeting wrought.—

Let Pavia make a captive king,
    And Rome a captive Pope ;
And cause his fame world-wide to ring,
    Beyond his utmost hope.—
"Good Monk! thou goest now determined stand to make ;
The like, nor I nor any valiant knight,
In our most earnest, doubtful, desperate fight,
    Can ever, and have never made !
If but thine aims are true God will not thee forsake.
Sure of thy course in His name, then, proceed,
And trust in Him to succour in thy need,
    Nor be at all of man afraid !"

This well-timed welcome Luther's courage fired,
    The next few steps into the presence led ;—
What at the Diet there at Worms transpired
    The whole world knows, no more need now be said.

But George of Freundsberg little knew
How much his words
With the great grand result had there to do ;
He little thought
When he the victory wrought,
When the Ticino whelm'd sad Pavia's beaten
hordes,
As his fierce charge
Of German lanzknechts swept the bloody field,
And chivalrous Francis forced to yield—
Or when at large
Through Rome's breach'd barricades, o'er the dying
and the dead,
With Charles of Bourbon he his stormers led—
In those his hours of victory,
Flush'd with success, he little, little dream'd,
While the fierce light of battle gleam'd,
And animation fired his eye,
His glorious feats would be forgotten ere
The cheering words that he had spoken there,
When on the Monk his glance in kindly welcome
beam'd.

Luther and Freundsberg! These are greater names,
    Associated now,
Than he as conqueror at Pavia claims,
    Though crown'd with victor's laurel-bough;
For by this speech he dealt a deadlier blow
    At the fell power of Papal Rome,
Than when in storm he laid her ramparts low,
    In tumult charging home.

THE MIDSHIPMAN AND THE BELLE OF THE BALL.

"My heart, my heart is free
　As my frigate on the sea,
　　Scudding merrily."
"Your frigate is a lifeless thing,
　'Tis a faulty simile!"
"As a sea-bird, then, upon the wing,
　Emblem of liberty!"

"But mine is freer still,
　As the butterfly at play
　With the warm sun's quickening ray,
　The livelong summer day
　　Sporting at will.

"What! and as fickle do you say?
　Then, sir, you shall have your way.
　　Whole—entire—without a care—
　　Freer than the joyous air
　　All-pervading—everywhere,—
My heart is free, is free, and gay."

"Gay sweetheart, if thy heart is free,
　　　Yield it me,
　　And in return take mine;
A bargain shall the transfer be,
　　The interchange divine—
　Thou with mine, as I with thine,
　Shalt hold me, as I hold thee,
　　By a token and a sign,
　　　By this—and this—
　　In fond captivity."—
Aye, the sailor-lad is free and bold,
　　Bold to woo and free to kiss.
He has circled her waist with a closer hold,
And she in a whisper her love has told,
　　　And she is his.

THE EMPEROR AND THE ABBOT.

(*From the German of Bürger.*)

I WILL tell you a tale, it is witty enough!
There was once a Kaiser, he was crusty and rough;
There was, too, a Lord Abbot of high degree,
'Twas a pity his shepherd was wiser than he!

Now the Kaiser must bear both the heat and the cold,
Sleeping oft in his mail in his mantle enroll'd;
Black bread and water full often he cursed,
And, oftener still, suffer'd hunger and thirst.

But the Abbot enjoy'd ever jolly good cheer,
And he loved both his bed and his board, never fear!
Like the full moon shone his oily fat face,
Nor could any three men his body embrace.

THE EMPEROR AND THE ABBOT.

So a grudge to the Abbot the Emperor bore—
And it happen'd one day as he rode to the war,
His train at his back, in the sweltering heat,
The Abbot he spied, lounging cool on his seat.

Ho ! chuckled the Kaiser, the luckiest chance !
Here with my fat Abbot I'll now break a lance :
" Holy Father, how are you ? It certainly seems
What with fasting and praying your countenance
  beams.

" But still must I think that your time passes slow,
And that you would thank me some work to bestow ;
You *are* the cleverest man out, or I'm sold,
The grass you can hear as it grows, I am told.

" So three innocent nuts I now put in your cheek,
And the answer in three months' time will I seek ;
To crack them a pastime—to give you more law
Would be quite thrown away, for you've got a strong
  jaw.

"First—When by my robes as the Emperor known,
With princes in council surrounding the throne,
How much I am worth to the uttermost mite,
Like a treasurer true you will answer aright.

"Reckon up, for the second, until you have found
How long it will take me to ride the world round,
To the minute exact, not too long nor too short;
The answer, in truth, to *you* is mere sport.

"The third: You shall guess, for of prelates you're prize,
To a hair what I think, my Lord Abbot most wise;
If you're right I'll confess it, but still, do you see,
Not an atom of truth in my thought must there be.

"But should it so happen my nuts you can't crack,
To be Abbot much longer the time you shall lack;
On an ass I'll command you be led through the land
Face backwards, the tail 'stead the reins in your hand."

The Emperor turn'd, full of laughter, and rode.
Out fuller than ever his cheeks the Monk blow'd,
Scratch'd his pate, plagued his brains, heaved sigh
    upon sigh,
Felt as though just condemn'd on the gallows to die.

He, one, two, three, four learned Faculties tasks,
Of one, two, three, four Universities asks,
And promises dues and fees not a few ;
But there is'nt a Doctor can answer him true.

And the time, how it runs ! while the answer he seeks,
The hours grow to days, and the days grow to weeks,
And the weeks grow to months, and still the time
    flies,
The Abbot grows yellow and green round the eyes.

And now see him, a pale, a lean, wasted old man,
Seek in woods and in fields to find peace if he can ;
He walks in a rocky, unfrequented way,
Where meets him Hans Bendix, his shepherd, one day.

"Lord Abbot," says Bendix, "what gnaws at your
    heart?
You waste right away, from yourself you will part:
By'r Lady and Joseph! your course will be run,
Unless, by my faith, you can get something done."

"Ah! good my Hans Bendix, 't must even so be,
For the Kaiser, he bears me a grudge, don't you see!
He has put 'tween my teeth three such nuts for to
    crack,
Can't be done were Beelzebub's self at my back.

"First: When by his robes as the Emperor known,
With princes in council surrounding the throne,
How much he is worth, to the uttermost mite,
Like a treasurer true I must answer aright.

"I must reckon the second until I have found
How long it will take him to ride the world round,
To the minute exact, not too long nor too short,
The answer to me *in truth* is mere sport!

"The third—was e'er prelate before so distress'd?—
To a hair what he thinks, he says, must be guess'd;
If I'm right he'll confess it, but still, do you see,
Not an atom of truth in his thought must there be.

"And should it so happen his nuts I can't crack,
To be Abbot much longer the time I shall lack;
On an ass he'll command I be led through the land,
Face backwards, the tail, 'stead the reins, in my hand."

"Is that all?" says Hans Bendix, with laughter full sore,
"The riddles to guess, good my lord, do not pore;
I can make it all right if you but lend to me
Your mitre and crozier and frock, do you see?

"For though I don't understand Latin a bit,
I am none the less proud of my own mother wit,
What you, all your learning, your gold, cannot gain,
I, leave it to me, will engage to obtain."

The Abbot he jump'd with delight, and he ran
And fetch'd mitre, and crozier, and frock, and began
Hans Bendix as Abbot to dress for the Court,
Where he sent him, and Bendix the Emperor sought.

The Kaiser he sat on the Emperor's throne,
And he lorded it high with his sceptre and crown;—
"Now tell me, Lord Abbot, like treasurer true,
How much am I worth? mind you give me my due."

"For thirty broad pieces Our Lord was betray'd!
Howe'er high you lord it, I'm therefore afraid
Twenty-nine's all you're worth, do not think it too
      few,
Surely *He* must have been worth *one* more than you."

"There is something in that," said the Kaiser aside,
"And it goes a long way to humble our pride;
But still I must own I am struck of a heap,
I had never believed I had gone so dirt cheap!

THE EMPEROR AND THE ABBOT.

"Now tell me the second: I suppose you have found
How long it will take me to ride the world round,
To the minute exact, not too long nor too short:
Methinks you can hardly turn this, too, to sport!"

"My Liege, with the sun if you saddle and ride,
And as fast as he goes but keep pace at his side,
I'll wager my mitre and crozier thereon
That in twenty-four hours the task will be done."

"Ha, ha!" laugh'd the Kaiser, "most splendidly put,
Your horses you feed with your 'if' and your 'but,'
With your 'but' and your 'if' he who maketh his pun,
Hath well fed his steed, *he* can race with the sun!

"Well! we'll pass to the third, and you'll need all your wit
If I'm not to condemn you face backwards to sit:
Of my thoughts that are false just one you shall find—
Your 'but' and your 'if' you will please leave behind."

"Your Majesty thinks me the Abbot!" "I do—
But the thought is not false." "My Liege, it's not true.
The hood makes not the monk, yourself you deceive,
I'm his shepherd, Hans Bendix, my Liege, by your
leave."

"The Devil!" cried the Kaiser, "you're not, as I see,
The Abbot, but henceforth the Abbot you'll be";—
Had he dropp'd from the skies 'twere no greater
surprise,
Yet a merry, bright twinkle broke out in his eyes—

"For I will reward you with crozier and ring,
Your predecessor backward in saddle I'll fling,
And there he will learn, as is proper and right,
To labour to live—it will be a rare sight!"

"My Liege, you're too fast, my day has gone by,
Neither read, nor yet write, nor figure can I,
Nor my life to save, could I speak aught of Latin,—
What the boy neglects the man ne'er can be pat in."

"Ah, honest Hans Bendix, that same's sure a pity,
Any favour I'll grant you, your jests are so witty;
I've been much entertain'd by these lusty, mad pranks,
They have earn'd you my praise, they deserve now my thanks."

"So please you, my Liege, I have no need of pelf,
But if I may ask any favour myself,
Then let me just beg, as my wish'd-for reward,
You will graciously deign to pardon my lord."

"Bravo, now, you knave! Your heart I can see
Is placed like your head e'en where it should be;
And, since you request it, we'll pardon your lord,
And grant you free quarters for life for reward.—

"Upon the Lord Abbot this ord'nance we lay,—
No more shall Hans Bendix keep sheep from to-day,
But the Abbot shall keep him in board and in bowl,
And when he shall die sing a mass for his soul."

NORFALL'S TOWER.

(*From the German of Trinius.*)

" What drives you, Wand'rer, out in the storm,
When your bed is so soft, your chamber so warm?
It has struck twelve already on Norfall's tower,
It pours so with rain, the winds rage in power."

" Are not *you* alarm'd, Watchman, by this howling
    blast?
And just see how the rain in pailfuls is cast.
'Fore ever the east to the dawn shall give birth,
Surely Norfall's Tower must fall crushing to earth!"

" Wand'rer, you may safely return and be quiet;
Know, it is nought but the Cloud-king's riot.
The Cloud-king, his revenge he can never forget;
He returns every year at the season set.

NORFALL'S TOWER. 75

"And thus it all happen'd:—As one evening he hied,
On the storm-wind's wings, from Thule's wild tide,
Round Norfall's Tower loud roaring he flew,
A maiden he saw the clear window through.

"Her look and her gestures her pride betray'd,
With wrath her mouth swell'd, reply scornful she made;
At her feet so sad, so anxious he felt,
So loving his look, a young lord knelt.

"'Oh, with pitying eye encourage my flame!
If I *am* audacious, who can the fault blame?
Who sees once your charms and feels not their pow'r,
Oh! who has a heart, but it's yours from that hour?

"'Yes, I adore you, I confess it, and say,
Dream of *you* the whole night, think of *you* the whole day.
Lofty Ideal! not hope I to prove
With you the joys ever of earthly love.

"'The pilgrim, he wends to Our Lady's seat,
Kisses the threshold, falls down at her feet,
And touches from 'far her heavenly dress—
Thus, Lofty Ideal! my suit would I press.'

"Proudly and coldly the youth she surveys,
'Up to me your eye how dare you to raise?
Know, many a king from the northern land
Has sought, but in vain sought, to win my hand.

"'Go, hide you, audacious! Let *his* spirit hiss
In death whose lips threat my hand but to kiss!
My hand shall not own mortal man that is dust;
My beautiful self ne'er to man will I trust!

"'Queen of the elves in the dale be my fate,
Or king of the sylphs of the air will I mate:
If *he* my double command can't obey,
Me *he* shall not force in his realms to stay!'"

"No sooner the words from her lips they have flown,
Than shakes Norfall's Tower: with sceptre and crown
There stands the Cloud-king, in boisterous storm,
In thunder and lightning, before her pale form.

"'High are your thoughts! To you shall be given
The lot for which you, dauntless, have striven.
You to woo, 'tis no use for this trembling worm,
I bring you a bride's gift of thunder and storm.

"'As you so rashly did swell in your pride,
Cloud-king will carry you home as his bride;
If *he* your double command can't obey,
He shall not force *you* in his realms to stay!'

"He speaks, and carries on whirlwind's arm
His struggling booty, despite her alarm,
Till, high in the air her vibrating ear
Her true lover's wails no longer can hear.

"At length in his palace he sets her down,—
The Sprite she coaxes, her arms round him thrown,
'You must now to your fellow-spirits, sweetheart,
My marriage proclaim,—let them, too, bear their part.'

"Three times he turns him in whirlwind: he's ta'en
Three hairs from his beard that's sodden with rain,
Three drops of blood thereon see him dash,
He welds them together with lightning's flash.

"Behold! they come.—Upon dripping steed
A white rider through the air does speed;
His mother behind, an ancient wight,
A shell all of pearl she brings to the light.

"'Cloud-king, all hail! To the feast, see, I bring,'
Says the King of the Waters, 'a rare new thing;
'Tis pretty miller's daughter's purple blood,
For I pull'd her down deep beneath my flood.'

"A carriage behold!—its wheels softly hum,—
Erl-king and his daughters, see, they come;
The elves of the dale ride on crickets around,
And lash the night-mares till the whips resound.

"'Cloud-king, all hail! To the feast, see, I bring,'
Says Erl-king with his daughters, 'a rare new thing:
It is a boy's heart still beating and warm!
Him caught I and slew on his father's arm!'

"Again was a hum, and a crackle thereto—
Glowing red dragons, snorting, him drew—
Behold! Salamander enveloped in flame,
And fierce tongues of fire, to the banquet came.

"'Cloud-king, all hail! So you sit at repast!'
Cried loudly the Fire-king, 'and I come the last.
Then serve up the maid—come, cheery to meal;
The Fire-king's hunger she'll only steel!'

"Loud shrieks Romhilda, with dread distress,
Alone in this terrible wilderness,—
'So! that's she who so rashly spirits would wed,
On her will we Sprites of the Waste be fed!

"'Aye, sweet! your hands you may wring till they bleed,
And wring them in vain; it is ever decreed,
That she who would be by us spirits embraced,
Her blood shall we suck, her flesh shall we taste.'

"'Nay, monster! Fulfil not that horrid decree
Before you have loosen'd the pact made with me,
If *you* my double command can't obey,
You cannot force *me* in your realms to stay.'

"'Ha, sweet! that won't make our soup even cold,
Command, and I'll do it as soon as told!'
She thinks, and again thinks,—her mind's in a whirl;
But at last she speaks out, poor trembling girl.

"'Of lovers the truest now fain would I see.'
And there stands her youth, indeed it is he:
On his loving heart her heart does she rest,
And tightly she presses him close to her breast.

"'You've shown me the truest of lovers; but still
You must show me a truer, ere you will fulfil
My double command!'—With frightful crash
The goblins vanish in lightning's flash.

"The morning sun disperses the gloom;
Peaceful Romhilda sleeps in her room,
And clasps in her arms her youth so true,—
Her hand and her life are well his due.

"Whene'er the autumn clouds fly fast and low,
Her window yet haunts her ancient foe;
Then let him roar as fierce as he will,
When the morning breaks he must be still."

COUNT EBERSTEIN.

(*From the German of Uhland.*)

The Palace at Spires rings with music and dancing,
By torchlight and waxlight there bright eyes are glancing;
    Count Eberstein
    Leads forth the line
With the Kaiser's daughter, so fine, so fine.

As he swings her round lightly, her heart he does gain,
And she whispers him softly, she cannot contain,
    " Sir Count, beware !
    Take care ! Take care !
Your castle to-night 'gainst the foe prepare !"

"Oh, I see," thinks the Count, "that's Your Majesty's
grace,
'Tis for this in the dance you have found me a
place!"
He seeks his steed,
His knaves doesn't heed,
But rides to his jeoparded castle with speed.

Echoes Eberstein fortress with fierce battle-din,
Up their ladders they try in the mist to get in :
Count Eberstein
Has welcome fine,
Casts them down off the walls along the whole
line.

The Kaiser rides over with the first morning
light,
Supposing the castle was taken in the night ;
But on the wall
With scorn they call
Out against him, Count, and merry men all.

Sir Kaiser, would you try 'gain castles to surprise,
How to tread a blithe measure you'll learn if you're
wise.
Your girl's a belle—
Dances so well,
To her my castle I'll willingly sell."

Rings Eberstein's castle with music and dancing,
By torchlight and waxlight there bright eyes are
glancing ;
Count Eberstein
Leads forth the line
With the Kaiser's daughter, so fine, so fine.

As he swings his bride lightly, her heart he will gain,
And he whispers her softly, he cannot contain,
"Maiden, beware !
Take care ! Take care !
Your castle to-night 'gainst the foe prepare !"

BERTRAN DE BORN.

(From the German of Uhland.)

HIGH upon the steep rock smoking
   Autafort's in ruin rent,
And its lord in iron fetter'd
   Stands before his sovereign's tent.
"Thou with sword and song so gifted,
   Hast thy talents foully spent;
Uproar in my lands hast foster'd,
   Children 'gainst their parents sent.

"Now thou stand'st in chains before me!
   Thou the proud boast yet shalt rue,
That to thee 'twas never needful
   E'en with half thy powers to sue!
Now the half shall not suffice thee,
   All thy talents are too few
To rebuild thy shatter'd castle,
   Or to break thy chains in two!"

"As thou sayest, Liege and Sovereign,
    Here I stand, Bertran de Born;
He whose single song enflamèd
    Perigord and Ventadorn,
He who to the mighty tyrant,
    In his side was aye a thorn,
Out of love to whom king's children
    Father's dreadful wrath have borne.

"In thy palace sat thy daughter,
    Feasting as the Duke's glad bride;
But my herald sang before her,
    Whom I did my song confide;
Sang her minstrel's hymn of longing—
    Hymn that once had been her pride—
Till she dew'd her bride's apparel
    With her tears—a streaming tide.

"In the olive's sleepy shadows
    Thy dear son my song did hear,
As with wrathful battle-music
    I bestorm'd his list'ning ear.

Quickly harness'd he his charger,
    And I did his banner rear,—
Till at Montfort's gate in battle
    Pierced his breast the hostile spear.

"As he in my arms lay bleeding,
    Not the sharp steel's throbbing pain,—
But to die by thee accursèd
    Caused his eyes their tears to rain.—
For he wish'd he could stretch to thee
    Right hand o'er the land and main,—
But as thine he could not reach to,
    Press'd he mine yet once again.

"Then, like Autafort above us,
    There my talents all were rent;
Nor the whole, nor half remainèd,—
    Harp and sword away I sent.
Easy thou mine arm hast fetter'd,
    Since my soul's in sorrow pent;
Only in this plaint so woeful
    Can I rouse me—I am spent!"

And the King's fierce brow relaxes:
"'Thou my son hast led astray!
Hast my daughter's heart bewitchèd!
Mine, too, hast thou touch'd this day.
Take mine hand, friend of my dead son—
Pardon dare I not delay.—
Burst those fetters!—Of thy genius
I have felt a powerful ray!"

THE YOUNG LORD AND THE MILLER'S MAID.

(From the German of Goethe.)

" Why want to pass,
   Pretty miller's lass,
     What's your name ? "—" Lizzie."
" But why want to pass,
     With the hay-rake in your hand ? "
   " On my father's land
   I am very busy."
" Do you go alone ? "—
" The hay is all mown,
That's the meaning of the rake ;
   In the garden close by
   Whether the pears are ripe I'm to try,
And a basket take."
" Is that not a grotto under the tree ? "
" There are two, don't you see ?

There's one on each side."
  " I'll come to you soon—
  And we will this hot noon,
 Together in the grotto hide ;
   Surely there in the green secluded place—"
    " Fie, what *would* people say ! "
   " Quite undisturb'd can we embrace."
    " Get away !
He who kisses the pretty miller's maid
Is straightway on the spot betray'd.
  Your beautiful dark cloth
  I were loth
    With flour to soil.
  Like unto like, that's the right plan,
   For me 'tis better through life to toil—
  Listen ! I love the miller's man,
   He wears nothing that I can spoil."

THE YOUTH AND THE MILLSTREAM.

(*From the German of Goethe.*)

YOUTH.

"Why hurry you away so fast,
    Brisk in flow?
Why so light-hearted rush you past
    Down below?
Clear brook, what is it that you seek
In the dale? Listen, for once, and speak."

BROOK.

"Friend, I was once a merry rill,
    But my pranks
Are ended now. Down to the mill,
    Within banks,
They've turn'd my former rushing course:
I'm always full, and run with force."

Youth.

"And you flow on, so calm in mood,
  To the wheel!
You know not what my young, hot blood
  Here does feel!
The miller's daughter's eye is cast
Upon you oft, as you run past."

Brook.

"Casement she opes at morning dawn,
  Comes to lave
Beautiful face and lovely form
  In my wave.
Her bosom is so white, so round,
I'm set on fire, am steaming found."

Youth.

"Can she kindle in water's flood,
  Love's hot flame?
Then, if no rest finds flesh and blood
  Who can blame?
For he who's seen but once her face
Must after her for ever race."

THE YOUTH AND THE MILLSTREAM.

BROOK.

"Myself upon the wheel I fling
    In fluster,
And all the paddles round I wring
    In bluster;
Since I the busy maid have seen,
My water-power has greater been."

YOUTH.

"You'll feel the pang like every one.
    She will say,
Partly in scorn, partly in fun,
    'Get away!'
She had the power to stop e'en you,
Chose she with love glance but to woo."

BROOK.

"From her myself I scarce can force;
    My wave flows
In twists and turns, in languid course,
    Through meadows;
And could I only have my will,
I would flow back to her uphill."

Youth.

"Companion of my deep love-pain,
I must go,
With joy you'll ripple oft again
As you flow.
Go tell her now, in whisper soft,
That still I hope, and tell her oft."

THE COUNT DE GREIERS.

(*From the German of Uhland.*)

STILL stands young Count de Greiers before his ancient hall,
And on the distant mountains his looks with longing fall;
In golden ray all glorious their rocky crests are seen,
And in the dawning twilight the Alpine vale between.

"Oh, Alpine heights so verdant, what power do ye possess!
Blest are your gay frequenters, cowherd and shepherdess!
Across I've gazed full often, and felt nor pain nor charm,
To-day desire o'ercomes me, my heart I cannot calm."

Close, and yet closer sounding, reedpipes enchant his ear,
The cowherds and their maidens now to the keep draw near,
And dance before the castle upon the lawn so light;—
Their wreaths and ribbons flutter, their white arms gleam so bright.

The youngest of the maidens, lithe as a twig of may,
Hold of the Count's hand catches before he can say nay,
Into the ring they force him, and whirl him round and round,
"Ho, ho! young Count de Greiers! a prisoner we have found!"

And off from thence they sprite him, in leaping dance and song,
They dance through all the hamlets, with swelling ranks along,

They dance the meadows over, they dance through
    forest glade ;
The distant Alps, in echoes, the joyous song
    repaid.

Has dawn'd the second morning, the third sun rises
    clear,
"Where is the Count de Greiers? Will he no more
    appear?"
And sultry now t'wards evening the sun sinks in his
    course,
It thunders in the mountains, the tempest gathers
    force.

And now has burst the storm-cloud, the brooks have
    swell'd to streams ;
And as the lurid lightning through the night's dark-
    ness gleams,
A man is seen in whirlpool, wrestling in desp'rate
    swim,
Till, snatching at a branchlet, he gains the eddies'
    brim.

"Here am I! Torn away from the mountain's joyous
    breast,
The storm in dance surprised me, I might not there
    live blest;
Found safety all the maidens in huts and rock's deep
    cleft,
But to the rainspout's mercy swept downward I was left.

"Farewell, green Alpine mountain, with thy so joyous
    band;
Farewell, farewell, blest three days spent in the shep-
    herd's land.
I was not born, alas not! such Paradise to share,
Heaven's wrath, in lightning flaming, found me in-
    truding there.

"And thou, sweet Alpine Rosebud! ne'er more touch
    thou mine hand,
I feel the wave, though ice-cold, hath not e'en
    quench'd thy brand;
And ye bewitching dances, enchant me ne'er again,
My father's halls receive me, safeguard me from such
    pain."

DURAND

(From the German of Uhland.)

To the lofty castle Balbi,
    Durand with his harp is wending,
And his goal approaching joyful,
    All his power in song is spending.

There he'll find the sweetest maiden,—
    When he plays her eyes will glisten,—
Eyes cast down, so tender blushing,—
    Holding e'en her breath to listen.

In the court by lime-trees shaded,
    Taking stand, he now is playing,
And, in streams of clearest music,
    All his sweetest things is saying.

From the balconies and windows
    Nod in friendly greeting flowers,
But the maid his song should glamour
    Holds no window in the towers.

And a stranger passes by him,
    Turns on him his eye in sorrow :
"Rest the dead ! The Lady Blanca,
    Not to-day, nor yet to-morrow,—

"No, nor evermore you'll waken !"—
    No reply Durand has spoken.
Dim, alas ! his eye already,
    And his heart—his heart is broken.

But in yonder castle chapel,
    Where uncounted candles glitter,
Lies in state the minstrel's true love,
    Bright with flowers bedeck'd her litter.

Scarce their senses e'en believing,
　　How the people quake in wonder,
For they see the Lady Blanca
　　Burst the bonds of death asunder.

Blooming, see! she is arising
　　Out of slumber's deepest trances,
And her raiment in the waxlight
　　Splendid as for bridal glances.

As not knowing what had happened,
　　As though she were even dreaming,
Asks she, full of longing, kindly,
　　"Durand's songs were sweetly streaming?"

"Yes, those streams of song were Durand's."—
　　"Will he sing again?"—Ah! never—
He, the dead to life awakens,
　　Him can no one bring back ever!"—

*　　*　　*　　*　　*　　*

In the land of the perfected
  Durand wakes with eager longing,
Seeking her who's gone before him,
  Thoughts of love his breast are thronging.

Heaven he sees all wide expanding,—
  Vacantly the minstrel gazes,
"Blanca! Blanca!" cries he, yearning,
  Wandering through its empty mazes.

THE WANDERING BELL.

(*From the German of Goethe.*)

There was a child to church one could
    Not take, away he'd scramble,
And every Sunday still he would
    Find chance the fields to ramble.

His mother said, "The bell does ring,
    And that is to remind you
If you yourself to church won't bring,
    The bell will come and find you."

The truant thinks: "The bell is hung
    High up within the steeple"—
As he comes out of school it's rung,
    He goes not with the people.

The bell has ceased, it rings no more,—
  "My mother me would master:"
But how he's scared, behind it tore,—
  He ran, the bell ran faster.

How fast it ran I scarce can tell,
  It threaten'd him to cover;
He ran in terror, but the bell
  Did still above him hover.

But then a dext'rous turn he took,
  And in a proper hurry
To church he went, o'er hedge and brook;
  The bell him did not worry.

And every Sun- and Holy-day
  He thinks of this adventure,
And to the church he wends his way;
  No longer needs he censure.

THE SKELETON DANCE.

(*From the German of Goethe.*)

From the tower the warder look'd down at midnight,
    Look'd down on the graves where they lay;
The full moon made everything bright with its light,
    The churchyard is as clear as by day.—
See! a grave makes a move, a second, and then
They arise, here the women, and there the men,
    In their white and their fluttering shrouds.

Enjoyment they seek, their joints they will stretch,
    In rings they join hands; what a number!—
The poor and the young, the old and the rich,—
    But in dancing the shrouds encumber.
And as now there's no need their shame for to hide,
See! they shake them all off, and o'er the hill-side
    Wafts the wind the winding-sheets scatter'd.

How they lift up their shanks! their bones how they shake!
   And their features, how strangely contort!
Such a clipperty-clap the dancing does make,
   Like a rattle, tune of a sort.
The warder he laughs, for the sight is so queer,
The tempter close by whispers sly in his ear,
   " Filch me one of their shrouds for a joke!"

'Tis thought—'tis done. Up the tower with his prize
   The warder makes haste to go—
Still the moon lights up, shining clear in the skies,
   The shudderful dance below,
Till one after another, away they sneak,
Each one, in its shroud, its grave does seek,
   And under the turf all is quiet.

But one which is left trips and stumbles about,
   And fumbles and gropes in the graves;
But none of its friends has so put it to rout,—
   O'er its head in the air the shroud waves.

The tower-door it shakes, but backwards is cast;
The warder's in luck, for the hinges hold fast,—
    They are bless'd with the sign of the Cross.

Its shroud must be had if the grave shall it hold,
    To consider it has not much time;
The carving it seizes, the skeleton bold
    Up the tower begins now to climb.
All's up with the warder, poor devil, I fear,
For it clambers the scrolls, already it's near,
    It is just like a long-legged spider!

The warder's knees quake, and quivers his lip,
    Oh! the shroud had he left alone!
His last hour has come—with an iron grip
    It claws hold of the topmost stone.
The moon for a moment is hid by a cloud—
A thundering "One" the clock it strikes loud—
    The skeleton falls all to pieces.

THE CASTELLAN DE COUCY.

(From the German of Uhland.)

How the Castellan de Coucy
   To his heart his hand press'd tight,
As the Lady of Fayel
   Flash'd upon his raptured sight!
Ever since that self-same moment,
   All his minstrel music thronging,
Recking nothing what the subject
   Pulsed that heartbeat's sudden longing.

But his songs avail'd him nothing,—
   All his songs of love so sweet;
And the hope he dared not harbour,
   That his heart on hers should beat;
For if e'er her tender mind
   Pleasure found in melting song,
Unconcern'd, she little heeding,
   Pass'd with her proud lord along.

Then the Castellan determin'd
  He his breast would clothe in steel,
And thereon the Cross would fasten,
  That fierce heart beat not to feel.
He had now in Palestine
  Fought through many a long, hot day,
Pierced an arrow cross and armour,
  To his heart it found the way.

" Listen to me, page so trusty,
  When this heart has ceased its beating,
To the Lady of Fayel
  Thou shalt bear it with my greeting."
Thus by consecrated earth
  In the grave his limbs are press'd;
But his heart, his heart so weary,
  Must not come, alas! to rest.

Ready, in an urn all golden,
  Well-embalm'd the heart they bear,
And on shipboard goes the servant
  Who was trusted with its care.

Storms arise, the waves run higher;
    Flash the lightnings, topmasts break;
All their hearts with fear are beating,—
    Only one heart does not quake.

Shines again the golden sun;
    On the land they gaze their fill;
All their hearts with joy beat high,—
    Only one heart there is still.
Through the Forest of Fayel
    With the urn the page draws near;
Sudden sounds a lusty horn,
    Hunters shout in full career.

Out the bush a stag there runs,
    In its heart an arrow fleet;
See! it stumbles, rears, and falls,
    Dropping at the page's feet.
'Tis the Baron of Fayel
    Whose shaft has the stag's heart found,
And his shouting noisy crew
    Quickly do the page surround;

And the Baron's fellows fierce
    Haste to seize the golden urn ;
But the page steps back a pace,
    Them with his right hand doth spurn.
" 'Tis the heart of bold Crusader,
    'Tis the heart of minstrel gay,
Heart of Castellan de Coucy,
    Let this heart pass on its way!

" For in death this charge he gave me,
    When his heart had ceased its beating,
To the Lady of Fayel
    I should bear it with his greeting."—
" That same lady know I well,"
    Cries the knight who led the band,
Hastily the golden urn
    Snatching out the page's hand.

Hiding it beneath his mantle,
    Rides he from the forest forth,
And the cold, dead heart he presses
    To his own so hot with wrath.

Soon as he his castle reaches,
 Tells the cooks to do their part;—
With the venison he has slaughter'd,
 They're to dress a rare strange heart.

When with flowers it's ornamented,
 On a golden dish 'tis placed,
Where the Lady of Fayel
 With her lord the table graced.
To his lady now he hands it,
 Feigning there the lover's part,
" When in hunt I chance to slay,
 Aye to thee belongs the heart."

Hardly has the lady tasted,
 Than her tears involunt'ry flow,
And it seem'd as if her soul
 In that flood away would go;
But the Baron of Fayel
 Cried with laughter long and wild,
" People say that hearts of ringdoves
 Make one melancholy, mild.—

"How much more, then, my dear lady,
   This, which I've had dress'd—Come, tell—
Heart of Castellan de Coucy,
   Who knew how to coo so well!"
When the Baron thus had spoken,
   Other taunts had added choice,
Rose the Lady of Fayel,
   Said to him with solemn voice,—

"Thou hast done me great injustice;
   Thine my love's unchanging force;
But to eat of heart so noble
   Will my soul from thine divorce.
All do I now well remember,
   All he sang in time gone by;
And although in life I conquer'd,
   Now in death I captive lie.

"Aye, to death I e'en resign me;
   Ne'er at meal I'll bear my part;
Other food I may not eat of,
   Since I've tasted of that heart.—

"But on thee may God have mercy,
    With my latest breath I pray!"—
All this happen'd with the heart
    Of noble minstrel, minstrels say.

TRUSTY OLD ECKART.

(*From the German of Goethe.*)

"I WISH we were further! Oh! were we at home!
The Night-terror, it nears! They come—see, they
    come!
    I am sure 'tis the Sisters so weird.
As, all flying, they rove, us should they find here,
I very much doubt but they'll drink up our beer,
    Leave us nothing but empty pitchers."

Thus speak the small children as low they crouch down;
Now stands there before them a wrinkled old clown.
    "Keep, children, still,—now, mind you, keep still;
The Sisters so weird from their hunt will pass by;
Let them drink what they like, for *they* are so dry,
    And the witches to you will be kind.

As he said, so it haps; the Terrors draw near,
And so grey they look, and so shadowy here,
    And they sip, and they lap of the best.
The beer is all gone, and the jugs they are dry;
With riot and tumult the storm passes by,
    Spreads over the hills and the valleys.

The children, much frighten'd, run home as they can,
They are join'd on the way by the kind old man :—
    " You have nothing to fear, little dears,
Of whipping or blame; on your side will I fight,
And, whatever happens, I'll make it all right;
    But be silent, like good little mice.

" And he who advises, and he who commands,
In play delights ever to join children's hands,—
    'Tis your trusty old friend, Old Eckart.
Of the wonderful man you've often heard tell,
His wonders, for true, you have credited well,
    In future yourselves shall confirm them."

And so they reach home, and whatever their fate,
Their jugs they hand over, and silently wait,
    Quite expecting a whipping or blame.
See! an excellent beer their parents have found,
Already three—four times the glass has gone round—
    Yet the jugs do not come to an end!

The wonder it lasts till the following day,
And then how much longer? no doubt you will say,
    How long will the jugs so continue?
The children, they giggle, and hold their tongues fast,
But stammer, and stutter, and chatter at last;—
    The spell breaks, and the jugs they are dry.

When, now, my dear children, with countenance true,
Speaks parent, or teacher, or elder to you,
    Listen, then, and obey to the letter;
Hold your tongues all you can, and learn from this song,
That silence is good, but to chatter is wrong,
    And the jugs with good beer will keep full.

HARALD.

(*From the German of Uhland.*)

Follow'd by all his warrior train,
    Harald, the hero bold !
Through a dense wood, so wild and dark,
    Rides by the moonlight cold.

They captured banners proudly bear
    High in the wind, which sway.
In echoes, Victory's hymns they sing,
    Back from the mountains play.

What rustles, lurking in the bush ?
    What hangs upon the tree ?
What hovers in the air above ?
    And in stream's foam may be ?

What throws down flowers around them all?
   What sings such loving song?
What dances through the warriors' ranks?
   Vaults on the chargers strong?

What presses close and kisses sweet,
   And holds in tight embrace?
The sword takes off, pulls down from horse,
   Gives neither rest nor grace?

It is the airy elfin troop!—
   They prove resistless foes;
Already all the soldiers good
   In fairyland repose.

But he, the bravest, still remains,
   Harald, the hero bold!
For he is mail'd, from head to foot,
   In steel, so hard and cold.

His warriors all have disappear'd,
    There lie the swords and shields;
Their chargers, empty-saddled, range
    At will, in woods and fields.

Sorrowing greatly rides from thence
    Harald, in hero's pride;
He rides alone by moonlight cold
    Through the dark wood so wide.

Clear from the rock it bubbles forth,—
    He does from saddle swing;
He takes his helm from off his head,
    And drinks of the cool spring.

But hardly has he quench'd his thirst,
    Than powerless falls his arm;
Down on the rock he's forced to sit;
    He nods in slumber calm.

Upon the self-same stone he sleeps
  Hundreds of years, they say;
His head is sunk upon his breast,
  His hair and beard are grey.

When o'er the wood with lightning's flash
  The thunder-peal is roll'd,
Dreaming, he snatches at his sword,
  Harald, the hero old!

THE ELVES.

(From the German of Uhland.)

First Elf.

"Come and see, my elfin sisters,
   What a graceful mortal child!
Hasten all, before she scampers,—
   Such a gipsy's very wild."

All in chorus.

"Darling, join our fairy dances
Where the moonbeam brightly glances!"

Second Elf.

"You shall be my tiny partner,
   Weight not over fifty pound!
Small your feet and very nimble,—
   Dance then with us in the round!"

Third Elf.

" While I three count you can hover
    In the air with lightest leap.
Stamp upon the ground a little,
    So that we the time may keep."

All in chorus.

" Be not angry, little treasure ;
Blithely trip our moonlight measure ! "

Fourth Elf.

" Dearest sweet, can you laugh merry ?—
    Or by moonlight would you cry ?—
Well then, cry, and in tears melting
    In the air as fairy fly."

Fifth Elf.

" Is your diligence praiseworthy,
    And to work you're not too proud ?
Are your bride-sheets ready woven ?
    Have you also spun your shroud ?

Sixth Elf.

"Do you know with lard and butter
 How to make your pastry light?
Carry you on tips of fingers
 Pepper's, salt's proportions right?"

All in chorus.

"Dearest, we will question ever;
Mind you give us answer never."

Seventh Elf.

"Have you something on your conscience,
 Like so many maidens sad?
Know you aught of stolen kisses?—
 That indeed were very bad!"

Eighth Elf.

"Or are you betroth'd already?
 Have a bridegroom e'er so true,
Who's allow'd to take you walking
 Afternoons from one to two?"

NINTH ELF.

"Do you wear a ring on finger,
   Set in gold, a jewel bright?
'Tis a sign your lover's loyal
   If it presses finger tight."

TENTH ELF.

"Sweetest, you should not be naughty.
   Have you, as I fear, hot blood—
You must learn to outgrow temper,
   For in marriage it's not good."

All in chorus.

"Darling, join our fairy dances
Where the moonbeam brightly glances."

THE END.

www.ingramcontent.com/pod-product-compliance
Lightning Source LLC
Chambersburg PA
CBHW020118170426
43199CB00009B/560